Happy Father's
2001
With Love,
Quinn

Fly-Fishing

LIFE IS BUT A STREAM

Fly-Fishing

LIFE IS BUT A STREAM

Mark Hoff

Ariel Books

Andrews and McMeel
Kansas City

ISBN: 0–8362–2646–1

Library of Congress Catalog Card Number: 96–85931

Contents

Introduction

Why fly-fishing? Why pursue the art (or folly, as some would say) of casting an artificial fly to a wary fish when one could far more easily use bait or lures? To a fly fisherman the answers are self-evident: because only fly-fishing challenges the body, soul, and brain of the angler. Because no other kind of fishing offers such intoxication, challenge, transcendence, and frustration. Fly fishermen believe that every fisherman, in his or her heart of hearts, would like to be a fly fisherman. They insist that an angler who goes through life without learning

fly-fishing is like a gourmand who deprives himself of French food or a sports fan who ignores all sports but bowling.

There are other ways of catching fish, fly fishermen admit, but none calls for the same blend of skill and imagination, or offers the mystery, fascination, and excitement of fly-fishing. The motto of the fly fisherman might well be the comment attributed to Dame Juliana Berners in the fifteenth century: *Piscator non solum piscatur* ("There is more to fishing than catching fish").

History of Fly-Fishing

Although the first anglers almost certainly eschewed the difficult art of fishing with a fly in favor of the more direct use of a worm on a hook, fly-fishing can boast of a very long history. In the third century A.D. the writer Aelian offered this description of an encounter between fly fishermen and their quarry (in this case, the trout): "They cover a hook with red wool, and upon this they fasten two feathers . . . they drop this lure upon the water and the fish being attracted by the color becomes extremely excited, proceeds to meet it, anticipating from its beautiful appearance a most delicious repast; but, as with extended mouth it seizes the lure, it is held fast by the hook, and being captured, meets with a very sorry entertainment."

The known history of fly-fishing in England begins with the printing of the *Treatyse of Fysshynge With an Angle* in 1496. The author, Wynkyn de Worde, describes artificial flies then used to catch trout, some of which are still fished today. In the mid-seventeenth century, Izaak Walton and Charles Cotton wrote what is undoubtedly the single greatest classic of fishing literature, *The Compleat Angler.* Although Walton did not insist that his readers go out and fly-fish, his advice to "Be Quiet, and go a-angling" revealed his intention to make fishing a philosophy, or perhaps better said, to make a philosophy of fishing. Ever since then, angling writers have taken the liberty of becoming armchair philosophers in their discourses on the mysteries of fly-fishing.

Fly-fishing evolved over the centuries primarily as a means of catching salmon and trout, those wariest and most prized of freshwater game fish, whose diets consist chiefly of insects that can only be imitated by artificial flies. In Great Britain and in Ireland, where trout and salmon have been abundant for many centuries, fly-fishing originated as an elite sport accessible to those lucky few who were wealthy enough either to own a trout stream or to pay the fees required to fish trout and salmon streams, which were usually privately owned. Elaborate rules and customs developed, such as the tradition that a fly fisherman could cast only to a fish he could see rising;

simply dragging a fly through the water in hopes of catching a fish was against protocol.

When fly-fishing spread to the New World, it was freed from many of those Old World traditions, and Americans, true to their nature, began to innovate. New flies were created by laborious trial-and-error methods. New techniques and technologies were developed for the rougher and wilder American rivers. Fly-fishing also became more democratic. With so much fine fly-fishing water in North America, the sport became accessible to more people, both rich and poor, and to women as well as men.

And if New World experimentation altered the methods of fly-fishing, it also broadened

the scope of the entire sport. Before the twentieth century, fly-fishing had been limited to trout and salmon, but American fly anglers, alert to the possibilities of their long coastlines, began to turn their gaze seaward toward heretofore un-fly-fished saltwater regions. What they found when they began catching ocean fish with flies was that many saltwater fish offered thrills every bit as great as those of trout and salmon. Today, saltwater fly-fishing is the fastest growing aspect of the sport.

Another development that profoundly changed the sport of fly-fishing occurred out of environmental necessity. Fly fishermen who worried about the environmental impact of their burgeoning sport began to advocate the adoption of "catch and release" fishing. This meant simply that fly-fishing was to be considered as a sporting contest in which one matched one's wits against the fish, and that after catching a fish one would release it unharmed. The idea of regarding fish as merely meat was to be rejected, suitable only for lowly bait fishermen. Today, the overwhelming majority of fly fishermen practice "catch and release" fishing.

The Gear

Anyone who has perused the pages of a fly-fishing catalog or wandered, Odysseus-like, through a fly-fishing store has seen to what absurd limits the fisherman's natural interest in gear and gadgets can be taken. For sheer variety of technical items and accoutrements, fly-fishing has no serious sporting rival. The vest of a well-equipped modern fly fisherman inevitably bulges with a bewildering array of specialized equipment: extra reels and fly lines; several spare leaders, carefully looped and stored in leather or plastic folders; hundreds of flies in various patterns, sizes, and colors, all organized in intricately divided boxes; pliers, hemostats, and special line cutters; thermometers to measure water temperatures; a large trout net and a small bug net; various sprays and floatants for flies, lines, or leaders; a clip-on flashlight; and, in the days of catch-and-release, a camera to photograph the fish that inspires the entire collection of equipment.

Contrary to what the incorrigible gear-hound may say, it was not always so. In the beginning, fly-fishing gear was simple: a rod perhaps six feet long, a line of grass or horsehair, and either a crude artificial fly or an insect tied or impaled on a hook. As centuries passed, however, fly fishermen, to their own selves being true, invented more gear to catch more fish.

The rod evolved from a relatively short stick of wood in the early days to the long, willowy poles (ranging from ten to twenty-two feet) used in the sixteenth and seventeenth centuries. By the late 1700s, the desire for more flexible rods that could cast farther with greater delicacy led to the use of split bamboo, in which several strips of bamboo were glued together to create a thinner and lighter rod that retained the integrity, resiliency, and strength of solid bamboo. A century later (1870 or so), hexagonal rods made from laminating six triangular strips of bamboo were manufactured in Europe and the United States.

Fly lines followed a similar course of evolution. For centuries, fly fishermen used horsehair; in the 1800s this was replaced by silk, which was coated with linseed oil that hardened into a waterproof coating. These new lines, which were quite expensive, cast more easily than horsehair and had the added versatility of being able to be fished as floating lines when greased or as sinking lines when ungreased. This made it possible to fish both with dry and wet flies. (The uninitiated will find an explanation of these terms in the next section.)

Reels were initially crude spools to hold line. From roughly the 1700s through the 1800s, mechanical innovations made the reel more reliable and efficient as a device not only to hold line but also to play a fish after it was hooked. By the late 1800s, one could recognize the forerunners of today's precision-machined reels.

As in all other things technological, the twentieth century brought profound changes to all aspects of fly-fishing gear. Rod manufacturers began to replace split bamboo with aluminum, then fiberglass, and finally carbon and graphite fibers. A modern nine-foot graphite fly rod weighs in at a mere two to three ounces,

and in the hands of an accomplished caster it can throw a modern synthetic line half the length of a football field. Today's fly reels are sleek, lightweight machines tooled from aircraft aluminum or even titanium.

Even clothing has been revolutionized by twentieth-century technology. Fly fishermen in England and Ireland may still fish in tweed jackets and caps, pipes stuck firmly in their

mouths, but the average American fly fisherman today is apt to be wearing the latest synthetic jacket, a pair of lightweight waterproof
neoprene waders with specially constructed
wading boots, polarized fishing lenses that en-
able fishermen to see fish better underwater,
and a vest made specifically for fly-fishing that
has already inspired imitators in the fashion
world.

Of course, the price tag for all these modern amenities may induce nostalgia for times
long gone. A well-heeled fly fisherman can easily step into the river with several thousand
dollars' worth of equipment on his back. At
that price, he inevitably attracts his share of
snickers from the lowly bait fishermen who

may share the same water at a fraction of the cost.

The advances of modern technology have also enlarged the fly-fishing world, for they have enabled fly fishermen to pursue game fish that were traditionally considered off-limits to the fly fisherman. Powerful saltwater fish like the tarpon, permit, barracuda, and even the mighty sailfish, which were previously fished almost exclusively with heavy spinning rods and reels, are now fair prey for fly fishermen equipped with the latest high-tech graphite rods, synthetic lines, large flashy streamer flies, and strong brass, aluminum, or titanium reels.

The Flies

Fly fishermen know—as do the fish—that of all aspects of fly-fishing, the most important is the fly itself. Flies are an undeniably complex matter: There are hundreds of thousands of fly patterns, with local, regional, and national variations on a given type. Specific patterns are always given names (the more colorful the better), with reference often made to the particular method used in tying it, the types of feathers or hair used, or the inventor of the pattern. Sometimes, as with old fly patterns, the derivation of a fly's special and unique name is lost in the murky depths of fishing history.

The most famous fly of all time is probably the Royal Coachman, a fly that imitates no known insect but whose distinctive patch of red has a powerful appeal to aggressive trout. The Royal Coachman also follows in the hallowed tradition of attaching colorful, even outrageous names to flies. Thus fly fishermen can pick from their bristling arsenals such bizarre creatures as the Grey Ghost, the Irresistible, the Lady Beaverkill, the Gold-Ribbed Hare's Ear, the Quill Gordon, the Hendrickson, the Royal Wulff, the Rat-Faced McDougal, the Mickey Finn, the Woolly Bugger, the Muddler Minnow, the Letort Hopper, or the Lefty's Deceiver.

Flies are generally grouped into four categories—dry flies, wet flies, nymphs, and streamers—though there is in fact a fifth. Dry flies, wet flies, and nymphs each imitate an aquatic insect at a different stage of its life, and so they represent the equivalent of one of the main food groups of trout or salmon.

The larval or nymphal stage is the infancy of an aquatic insect's life, so nymphs are used by fly fishermen to imitate insects at this immature stage, which constitute a large portion of a trout's diet. Nymphs are almost always fished with a sinking line or a weighted floating line under the water's surface or along the bottom of a stream or lake bed.

When nymphs grow into full-fledged winged insects, they float on the water's surface and then take to the air. Such adult insects are imitated by dry flies. When large hatches of these insects occur, trout may literally go into a feeding frenzy, gorging themselves on the floating insects. This represents something close to heaven for fly fishermen, especially those who regard dry–fly-fishing as the pinnacle of their sport. According to the aficiona-

dos, there is no thrill quite like that experienced when one delicately casts a dry fly to a feeding trout, then watches with nerves tingling as the fly floats along the water's surface, only to explode in a shower of water as a hungry trout rises up to seize it in his jaws. Enough has been written on the delicate and demanding art of dry-fly-fishing to fell a forest, and mastery of the art continues to evade all but the most dedicated of fly fishermen.

Wet flies, which have fallen from favor in modern times but once enjoyed tremendous popularity, generally come closest to representing drowned insects, although some trout probably mistake them for nymphs as well.

Streamers, which often have the most colorful displays of feathers of any fly, represent minnows and other baitfish. They can be especially deadly with larger trout but are often used to fish for other species as well, especially saltwater varieties. Saltwater fly-fishing is now attracting increasing interest from fly fishermen intent on pursuing the excitement of the larger and more powerful game fish than trout.

Finally, there are the terrestrials, which are imitations of ants, grasshoppers, and other nonaquatic insects that fall into the water and become trout food.

Fly fishermen not only have to worry about which type of fly pattern to select, they also have to select the right hook. Hooks are numbered by size; the smaller the number, the larger the hook. Large flies in sizes from 0 to 6 are usually used for large trout, salmon, and (especially) saltwater game fish. Commonly used trout flies range in size from 8 for larger nymphs and streamers to tiny 24 dry flies used in the most delicate presentations on small streams.

The Fine Art of Fly Tying

Any fly fisherman who has ever put feather to hook in hopes of creating a passable imitation of an insect or minnow will acknowledge that fly tying is an art in itself. Some of the world's most famous fly fishermen attained their fame as much for their fly-tying skills as for their fishing prowess. Indeed, flies created by the most famous and gifted tiers are often snapped

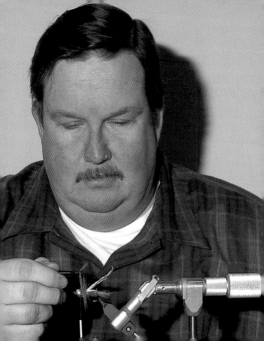

up by fly-fishing aficionados, who carefully store them under glass and wouldn't even think of allowing them anywhere near the brutish jaws of a hungry trout or salmon.

Yet as shrouded in mystery and mystique as it may be, fly tying is a hobby born of necessity for many fly fishermen, who can create their own flies at far less cost than professionally tied ones. (Flies that cost $1.50 apiece in a tackle store can be made for 10 cents at home.) Flytiers also simply enjoy sitting down after dinner to tie a few flies in anticipation of the next day's fishing. The tier's basic equipment includes a special vise to hold the hook, several spools of thread, lead wire, silver and gold tinsel, glue, and an assortment of "hackles" or feathers from chicken and rooster necks, as well as duck, pheasant, and peacock feathers and a variety of rabbit furs and deer hairs. Skilled tiers can easily assemble several thousand dollars' worth of tying equipment. Some fly-tying fanatics are even known to raise their own roosters, take up duck and deer hunting in order to assure their supply, and to scavenge roadkills for a good supply of their favorite furs and feathers!

The Fish

Although it is true that various freshwater and saltwater fish are pursued by fly fishermen, the quintessential fly-fishing game fish remain the trout and salmon. Here are several unscientific descriptions of the trout and salmon species most commonly pursued by fly fishermen.

Trout

Brown Trout (*Salmo trutta*). The brown trout can be considered the fly fisherman's trout par excellence, a trout made expressly for the fly angler. This speckled fish has been swimming around on the earth for some seventy million years. Native to Europe and North Africa, it first reached North America in 1882 when William Gilbert of Plymouth, Massachusetts, imported about five thousand brown trout eggs. Most of the eggs were infertile and did not hatch, and only three grew to maturity. Yet those three fish became the progenitors of a huge population of American brown trout. The brown trout is notoriously territorial, staking out an area in his waters and defending it ferociously. With a reputation as the smartest of all trout, the brown is notoriously difficult to catch, and is thus a favorite quarry of the famously masochistic fly fisherman.

Rainbow Trout (*Salmo gairdneri*). This fast-water fish is named for the brilliant red stripe that runs along its side. Native to a region stretching from the mountains of northern Mexico to the Aleutian Islands, the rainbow is now found throughout the continent wherever waters remain cold enough for it to survive. The rainbow is an aggressive fish, fierce when hooked, and known for its leaping abilities.

Rainbow trout that migrate from the rivers of their births to the sea or to large lakes are known as steelhead, which are famed game fish in their own right, and formidable travelers. Tagged steelhead that were stocked in streams in the eastern United States have been recovered by commercial fishermen in the Gulf of Mexico. Steelhead aficionados claim that their fish is the best fighter, pound for pound, of all the trout and salmon species.

Brook Trout (*Salvelinus fontinalis*). The beautiful brook trout is characterized by the red spots surrounded by blue circles on its sides. Native to northeastern North America, it has been introduced to the rest of the United States, Canada, South America, and Europe.

The brook trout, or "brookie," is not as adaptable as other trout, requiring very cold water, and has a reputation as an easier trout to catch than the brown, because of its less discriminate feeding habits.

Cutthroat Trout (*Salmo clarki*). Cutthroats get their name from the red streak along their lower jaws. They migrate to the ocean in their second or third year of life, and spend about

two years in the ocean before returning to rivers to spawn. Cutthroats are native to the western United States.

Salmon

The salmon is without doubt one of the premier game fish in the world. Prized both for its fighting ability and the exquisite taste of its distinctive red flesh, the salmon's mythic stature is enhanced by its mysterious ability to migrate from its freshwater birthplace in mountain streams and rivers to the oceans, whereupon it makes a long and laborious return trip, jumping upstream over waterfalls and swimming through rapids to spawn in its birthplace.

Atlantic salmon (*Salmo salar*). This is one of the most highly prized game fish in the world. Named by the ancient Romans for its jumping abilities (salar means "to leap"), the Atlantic salmon is highly prized by fly fishermen, although it is quite difficult to catch. Once hooked, this salmon does its name proud by leaping aggressively in order to shake the hook loose. The fish ranges the northern Atlantic Ocean from

Greenland to Cape Cod, and in Europe from Russia to Portugal.

Chinook salmon (*Oncorhynchus tshawytscha*). The chinook, the largest of the six species of Pacific salmon, is the king of salmon; fish over 125 pounds have been taken commercially. The rod-and-reel record is ninety-three pounds, but chinooks usually average fifteen to thirty-five pounds. Most chinook fry go to the sea, where they travel distances of over two thousand miles and feed on anchovies, herrings, crustaceans, and squid. After about five years they return to the rivers of their birth to spawn. They stop feeding upon entering fresh water, but will strike brightly colored lures and flies, perhaps out of anger.

Sockeye or blueback salmon (*Oncorhynchus nerka*). The sockeye range all over the northern Pacific Ocean and as far south as the Columbia River. Sockeye are small members of the Pacific salmon family; most of them average between four and eight pounds. Young sockeyes spend their first few years in the lakes in which they were born, and then migrate to the sea.

Coho salmon (*Oncorhynchus kisutch*). Cohos are among the most popular game fish of the Pacific Northwest. Found from California to Japan, they were also introduced to the Great Lakes, where they are now also fished extensively. Their average size is six to twelve pounds, but a record thirty-three-pound coho was taken in

1970 in Michigan. Cohos are unique among the Pacific salmon because they don't travel far from the rivers in which they hatch. Mature cohos feed in the ocean just off the mouth of their parent rivers.

Fly Casting

The first thing that nonfishermen inevitably wonder at when observing fly fishermen at work is the graceful work of rod and line during the process of fly casting. A fine fly caster can mesmerize onlookers as he lifts the line effortlessly from the water, flips it back and forth in tight loops over his head, and finally sends the weightless fly back over the water's surface to drift down silently and softly, mimicking the flight of an insect. Like fly tying, fly casting is an art in itself, and accomplished casters are often sought after by anglers wishing to learn as much as they can about these sacred mysteries.

Just as it is said that one can never set foot in the same river twice, so it may be said that no single cast is ever identical to the one that preceded it. Every fly fisherman has his or her personal style, and one of the great satisfactions of the sport consists in the physical pleasure of fly casting.

Personal preferences also extend to the kind of rod and line used. Some anglers prefer the strong, quick action of a modern graphite rod, whereas others swear by the slower and slightly heavier action of handmade bamboo fly rods. Regardless of the type of equipment used and despite much of the mystique surrounding it, fly casting is a relatively simple process. Because flies are virtually weightless, the line itself bears the weight that makes casting possible.

The caster lifts the line off the water with a flick of the wrist and a backward movement of the forearm. Simultaneously, the rod tip is shifted from roughly a ten o'clock position to two o'clock. The line sent backward over the angler's head slowly unrolls and extends itself almost horizontally to the ground. At the split second when the line is almost fully extended behind him, the angler flicks his wrist and forearm forward, reversing the line's direction and sending it shooting out in front. As the line extends over the water, the angler gently

lowers the rod tip and allows the delicate leader attached to the end of the line to uncoil and drop the fly gently on the water in front of the feeding trout.

Sometimes several "false" casts are made, in which the angler repeatedly casts the line back and forth in order to pull more line from his reel and cast out a longer length of line.

When all goes well, fly casting is a relaxing physical process that calms the mind, quiets the heart, and, with luck, fools the fish. But when all does not go well, casting can be the most frustrating activity ever invented. Leaders develop knots, which then multiply in nefarious ways, spoiling the presentation of the fly and requiring laborious untangling. Flies catch in everything imaginable: tree branches, rocks, weeds, clothing, and even the angler's own ears, head, or hands. Many doctors have stories to tell, humorous to anyone except fishermen, about fly hooks extracted from the oddest parts of the human anatomy. But the hazards of fly casting only add spice to the experience, and any fly fisherman will agree that the accumulated frustrations of bad casts only add to the pleasure and anticipation of the ultimate goal: a perfect cast over a perfect stretch of water to a perfect fish.

Great American Fly-Fishing Rivers

The main characters of fly-fishing stories are always the fish and the fly fishermen, usually in that order of importance, but one element more than any other creates the experience itself: the water. Famous fly-fishing waters have inspired legions of fly fishermen, writer and nonwriter alike, and more than one fly fisherman has ordered that his ashes be scattered over the surface of his favorite river. Thus, no account of the sport can hope to be complete without at least some mention of the waters that make it all possible.

The North American continent has always been extremely generous to New World fishermen, and perhaps to fly fishermen, above all others. Because fly-fishing evolved primarily as river fishing, the quintessential fly-fishing waters have been rivers. The first American rivers to gain fame among fly fishermen were in the Northeast, where the sport was first practiced in North America.

The Beaverkill

The Beaverkill and its sister stream, the Willowemoc, both of which rise on Doubletop Mountain in the Catskills, form one of the most famous trout fisheries in the United States. This is in large part because so many fishing writers described its waters before the Civil War. Theodore Gordon, known as the father of American fly-fishing and of the Quill Gordon fly, spent his last years on the Beaverkill, Willowemoc, and the Neversink. The Beaverkill is home to large quantities of very wily brown trout, and during spring and summer fly fishermen are often out on the water well before dawn to match their wits against these difficult trout.

The Battenkill

The Battenkill is a beautiful mountain stream that rises high on Bromley Mountain in Vermont and runs through the hills and valleys of that state before crossing into upper New York and dropping toward the Hudson River. The Battenkill supports large numbers of wild brook trout and brown trout.

The Letort and the Yellow Breeches

Spring creeks, so named because they originate in springs, are much loved by fly fishermen for their intimate charm and crystal-clear

water, and Pennsylvania's Letort and the Yellow Breeches are among the most famous spring creeks in the country. The Yellow Breeches winds through beautiful Cumberland County along its way toward the Susquehanna, and supports many smaller brown trout. The Letort was made famous by the fishing writer Vincent Marinaro, author of *A Modern Dry-Fly Code*, and is also known as the birthplace of the Letort Hopper, a grasshopper imitation that is a very effective fly.

Michigan's Au Sable

Another fly-fishing shrine is the famous Au Sable of Michigan. Early French explorers referred to it as La Belle aux Sables. This fine trout stream was well known long before the Civil War, and fly fishermen who make frequent pilgrimages there have referred to the Au Sable as "The Holy Water." Many of the fishing scenes in Ernest Hemingway's fiction describe Michigan streams such as the Au Sable, where Hemingway fished as a boy.

Montana Madness

Montana has become something of a mecca for fly fishermen, and many a dedicated angler from the East has uprooted family and career to be closer to the state's fabled rivers, recently immortalized in the film of Norman MacLean's

A *River Runs Through It*. Montana probably has more fine fly-fishing rivers than any other state, and each one has its devotees. A list of the names of the best known rivers is pure poetry to the fly fisherman dreaming of a fishing vacation. There are the Blackfoot, the Bitterroot, and the Clarks Fork near Missoula, along with the Missouri, the ever-popular Madison, the Smith, the Musselshell, the Beaverhead, the Gallatin, the Big Hole, and the Bighorn. All of these rivers boast of enough magnificent scenery, brown trout, and rainbow trout to make any fly fisherman's heart race with adrenalin.

Henry's Fork in Idaho

Named for Colonel Andrew Henry of the Rocky Mountain Fur Company, Henry's Fork of the Snake River is one of the world's most famous trout streams. Supporting abundant insect life on its banks, Henry's Fork is known for its plentiful insect hatches and its large rainbow trout. It is also notoriously difficult to

fish, because the insect life is so abundant there that the trout can afford to be extremely choosy about the types of insects they select, and so any fly fisherman who cannot "match the hatch," or duplicate the exact type of insect on the trout's menu will be out of luck. An angler was once seen to throw his expensive bamboo fly rod into the stream out of frustration at not catching any of the fish that were feeding greedily and happily around him.

Oregon's Umpqua River

Oregon's beautiful Umpqua River is famous for its steelhead trout, the oceangoing rainbow trout that are such magnificent fighters and

leapers. The Umpqua rushes down from the mountains toward the Pacific Ocean through conifer forests and along ledges of ancient lava. The silvery steelhead begin their runs up the river in spring and continue through the fall and early winter. Steelhead anglers who make pilgrimages to the Umpqua do so knowing that the fishing is difficult in its rough waters, but the river's beauty can be its own reward.

Alaskan Heaven

The mere mention of Alaska can cause fly fishermen to hyperventilate, as it conjures images of huge rainbow trout, leaping salmon, and the exotic grayling. Like Montana, Alaska has so

much great fly-fishing water that one can merely list the exotic names of its countless world-class rivers and lakes--the Kvichak, Brooks, Naknek, Kenai, Talarik, Alagnak, and Kulik Rivers, and Nonvianuk, Iliamna, and Tikchik Lakes.

These Alaskan waters offer some of the world's best rainbow and salmon fishing, as well as more unusual species, such as Dolly Varden trout and grayling, a beautiful fish with a very large sail-like dorsal fin, highly prized by fly fishermen. Rainbow trout that at two to three pounds are called large in the Lower Forty-eight are small fry in Alaska, where they can run over ten pounds and two feet long. Fly anglers in search of salmon can pursue the pink (or humpback), the beautiful sockeye with its crimson markings, the silver, chum, and coho, as well as the leviathan of the salmon world, the chinooks (or king salmon), which are so large and so strong (they can weigh in at over sixty pounds) that, once hooked, they are extremely difficult to bring to shore with fly-fishing equipment. With catches such as these, it is no wonder that many Alaskan fishing lodges are booked a year in advance.

The text was set in Celestial Antique and the
display in Ovidius Demi Bold by
Snap-Haus Graphics of Edgewater, N.J.

Book design by Diane Stevenson